Sitting Together
Activity Book

Sitting Together

....

Vol 1. Adult Study Guide
*Thirty-six lessons for adult learners
and for teachers working with children.*

Vol 2. Children's Lesson Plans
*Thirty-six lesson plans for children aged 3–12
and Songbook.*

Vol 3. Activity Book
*Fifty-seven coloring pages, puzzles, craft templates,
and more.*

Website: mindfulfamilies.org
*How-to videos, song audio files,
and downloads.*

Sitting Together

A FAMILY-CENTERED CURRICULUM ON MINDFULNESS,
MEDITATION, AND BUDDHIST TEACHINGS

···

Activity Book

Sumi Loundon Kim

Wisdom

Wisdom Publications
199 Elm Street
Somerville, MA 02144 USA
wisdompubs.org

Library of Congress Cataloging-in-Publication Data
Names: Loundon, Sumi, 1975– author.
Title: Sitting together: a family-centered curriculum on mindfulness, meditation, and Buddhist teachings: activity book /
  Sumi Loundon Kim.
Description: Somerville, MA: Wisdom Publications, 2017. | Includes bibliographical references.
Identifiers: LCCN 2016029073 (print) | LCCN 2016058382 (ebook) | ISBN 9781614291183 (vol 1: adult study guide
  (pbk.): alk. paper) | ISBN 1614291187 (vol 1: adult study guide (pbk.): alk. paper) | ISBN 9781614294191 (vol 2:
  children's lesson plans (pbk.): alk. paper) | ISBN 1614294194 (vol 2: children's lesson plans (pbk.): alk. paper) | ISBN
  9781614294245 (vol. 3: activity book (pbk.): alk. paper) | ISBN 1614294240 (vol. 3: activity book (pbk.): alk. paper)
  | ISBN 9781614294344 (vol. 3: activity book (ebook)) | ISBN 1614294348 (vol. 3: activity book (ebook)) | ISBN
  9781614291411 (vol 1: Adult Study Guide (ebook)) | ISBN 9781614294337 (vol 2: Children's Lesson Plans (ebook)) |
  ISBN 161429433X (vol 2: Children's Lesson Plans (ebook))
Subjects: LCSH: Buddhism. | Spiritual life—Buddhism. | Mindfulness (Psychology) | Meditation—Buddhism. | Buddhist
  families. | Buddhism—Study and teaching.
Classification: LCC BQ167 .L68 2017 (print) | LCC BQ167 (ebook) | DDC 294.3/444—dc23
LC record available at https://lccn.loc.gov/2016029073

ISBN 978-1-61429-424-5   ebook ISBN 978-1-61429-434-4

21 20 19 18 17
5 4 3 2 1

Cover and interior design by Gopa & Ted2, Inc.
Set in ITC New Baskerville Standard 10.3/15.

Printed in the United States of America.

Meditation Bell

Pinwheel Template

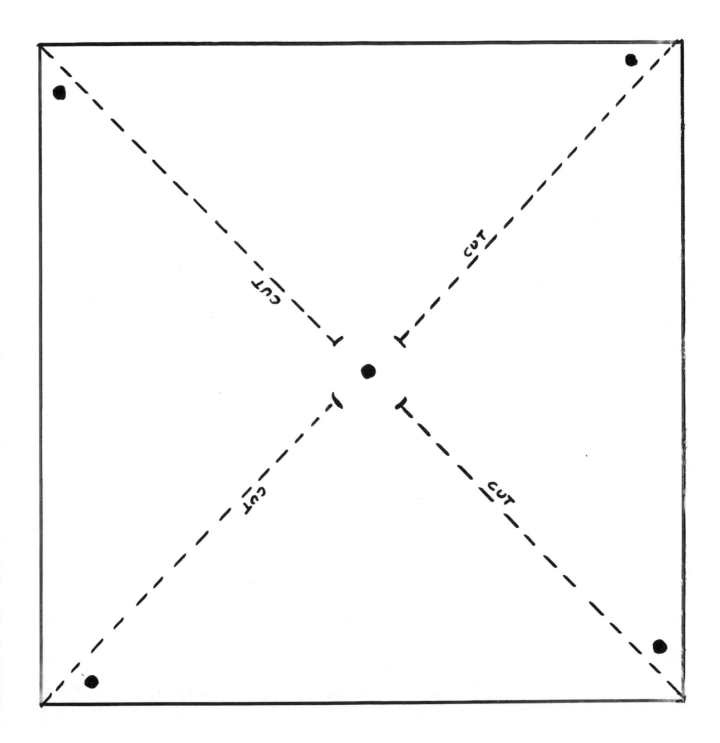

Six Senses House Template

Six Senses House Template 2

No Ordinary Apple

For use with Lesson 1.2 Meditation: Mindfulness of the Senses • *Line drawing by the author based on an illustration from* No Ordinary Apple: A Story About Eating Mindfully, *by Sara Marlowe and illustrated by Philip Pascuzzo.*

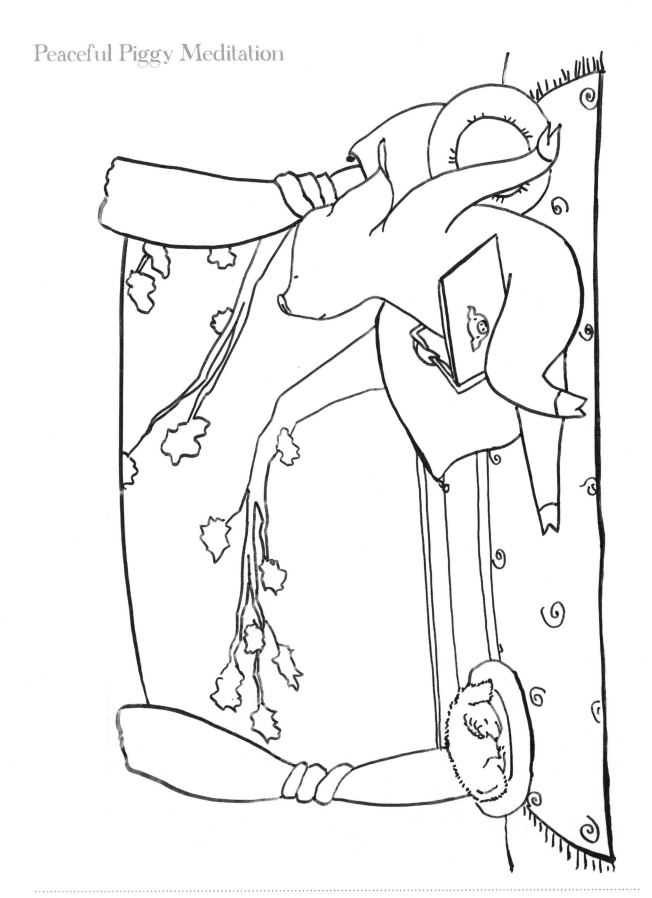

For use with Lesson 1.3 Meditation: Mindfulness of the Body • *Line drawing by the author based on an illustration from* Peaceful Piggy Meditation, *by Kerry Lee MacLean.*

Finger Walking Labyrinth

Directions for Finger Walking Meditation: Use one or two fingers from the hand you don't use for writing or drawing. Slowly trace your way through the corridors of the labyrinth. Breathe slowly and deeply. When you arrive at the center, then walk your way back out. Don't worry: you cannot get lost, as this is not a maze. You do not have to think or plan your route: the corridors will guide you.

Additional: glue yarn along the lines to create a three-dimensional labyrinth.

Moody Cow Meditates

Monkey Mind

Directions: Write or draw a series of four thoughts, each connected to the previous one. For example, "I want to build a space ship from this cardboard box. Then, fly to the moon. I will need some astronaut ice cream. Yum . . . ice cream . . . ."

Pebble Meditation

Stone Soup

Directions: Cut out soup ingredients and glue into the soup bowl.

For use with Lesson 1.8 Meditation: Stone Soup • *Illustrated by Pascale Lafond.*

Meditation Word Scramble

HREEATB

_____

AXLRE

_____

INMUDLF

_____

DOYB

_____

AOTNETITN

_____

TATIIODMNE

_____

NAWSERESA

_____

LAGIKWN

_____

BELEPB

_____

EENPRST

_____

TIEQU

_____

ECEULPAF

_____

Sunset

My Hideaway

Mice Sharing

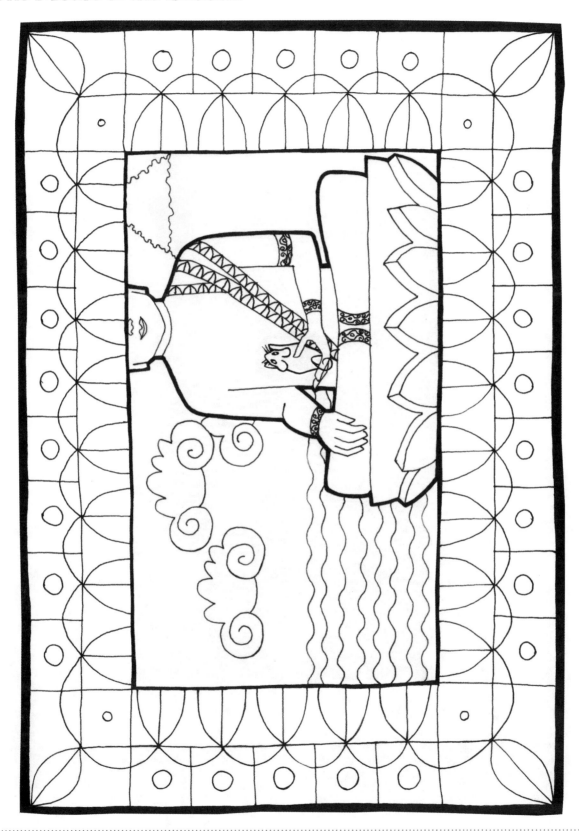

Fly Free

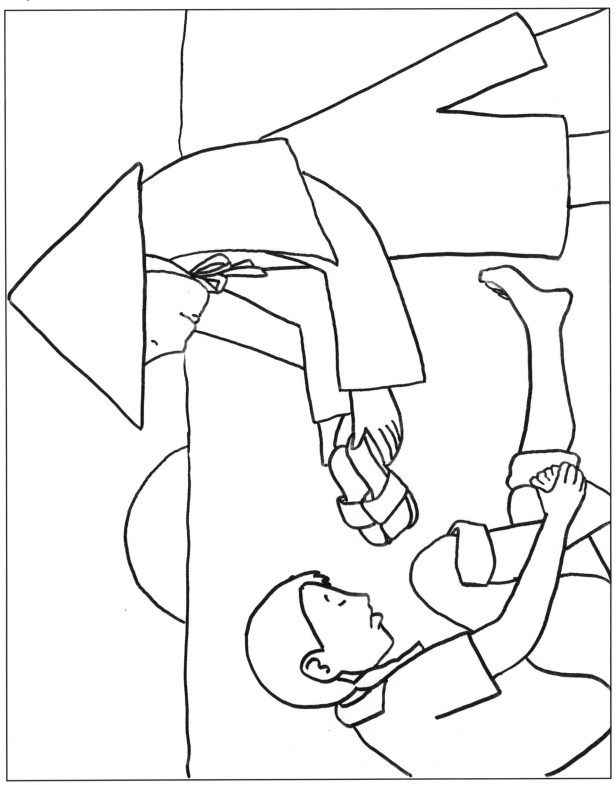

For use with Lesson 2.4 Kindness: Circle of Kindness • *Line drawing by the author based on an illustration*
from Fly Free! *by Roseanne Thong, illustrated by Eujin Kim Neilan.* © *2010 Roseanne Thong and Eujin Kim Neilan.*
Published by Boyds Mills Press. Used by permission.

Story Writing Template

My Meditation Space

Directions: Draw in your own face, hair, skin color, and clothing style. Draw treasures and other things that are precious to you to create your own altar. Decorate your meditation space to make it special to you.

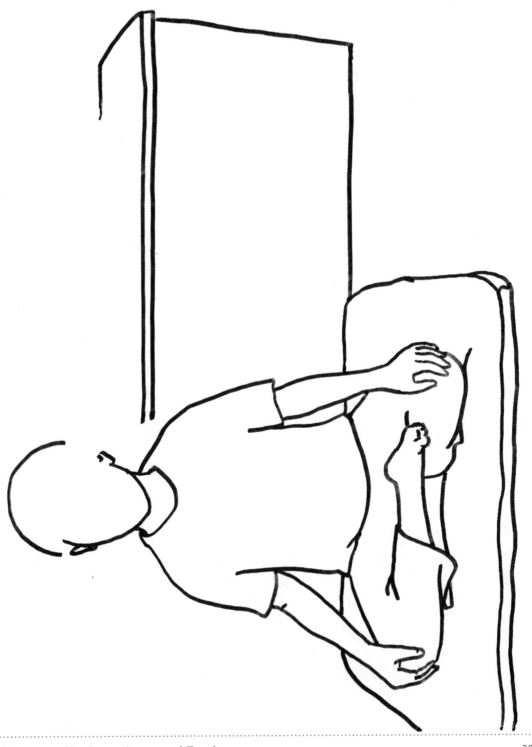

Zen Ties Crossword

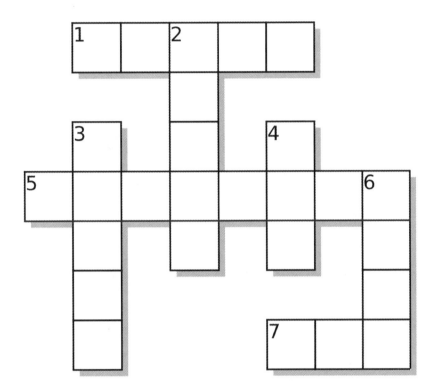

ACROSS

1 How Koo arrives and leaves
   (type of transportation).

5 The gift Stillwater gives to Koo
   at the train station.

7 What Koo keeps from his visit;
   used for drinking tea.

DOWN

2 Type of fruit Karl gives Miss Whitaker;
   she makes tea from them.

3 Stillwater is this type of animal.

4 Name of Stillwater's nephew.

6 The hot food the children cook for
   Miss Whitaker.

METTA

```
D L R O W R Q T B J Q M
Y P M G D M M D N D R T
M O O N L I G H T A R F
S H R D L E E B L M R D
R A S N N A V L Q I B F
E P P S L E B I E N A B
H P Y T E E L N G M Y Y
C Y H G I N D I I R M Y
A Y L N E S D L M E O L
E R G J V A Y N N S T F
T S T Y O F T E I J D R
L Y D R L E K J K K R T
```

KINDNESS	HEALTHY	FORGIVE
FAMILY	FRIENDS	ALL BEINGS
LOVE	TEACHERS	WORLD
SAFE	MOONLIGHT	SMILE
HAPPY	ENEMY	

For use with Lesson 3.1 Ethics: Overview • *Line drawing by the author based on an illustration from*
Kindness: A Treasure of Buddhist Wisdom for Children and Parents, by Sarah Conover and illustrated by Valerie Wahl.

Five Precepts

Ethics Worksheet for Children

Examples of when we...		Examples of when we...	
... support life		... kill or harm	
... share and be generous		... steal	
... are a good friend		... hurt others	
... speak and listen mindfully		... speak harshly, gossip, or tell lies	
... eat and play healthily		... eat or consume harmful stuff	

Moody Cow Learns Compassion Crossword

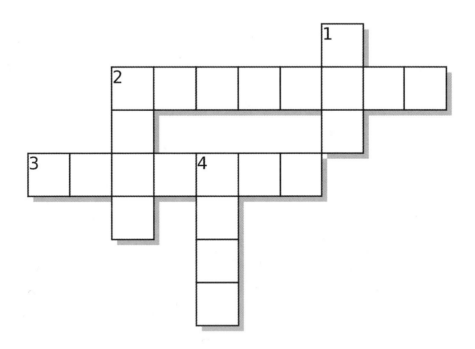

DOWN

1 Peter is this type of animal ("Moody ___").

2 Where the snake lives, has water (begins with letter *p*).

4 Name of Bully's snake.

ACROSS

2 Where grandpa got the crickets (two words).

3 Special glass bottle with water and sparkles that Moody Cow uses for meditation (two words).

Feeding Ducks

TUTHR

LSEI

SIOGPS

SPAEEL

OSYENTH

NSEIELC

PNSICSOAOM

ESIW

TLOEEENHP

SHNGIRA

Mindful Listening

My Healthy Body

Rainbow Fish Scales Activity Page

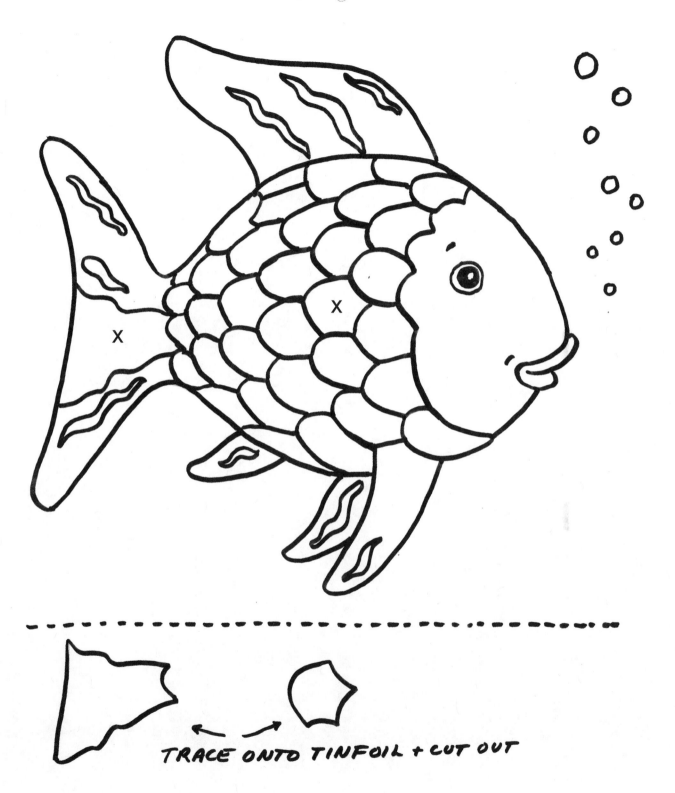

TRACE ONTO TINFOIL + CUT OUT

Quilt Template 1

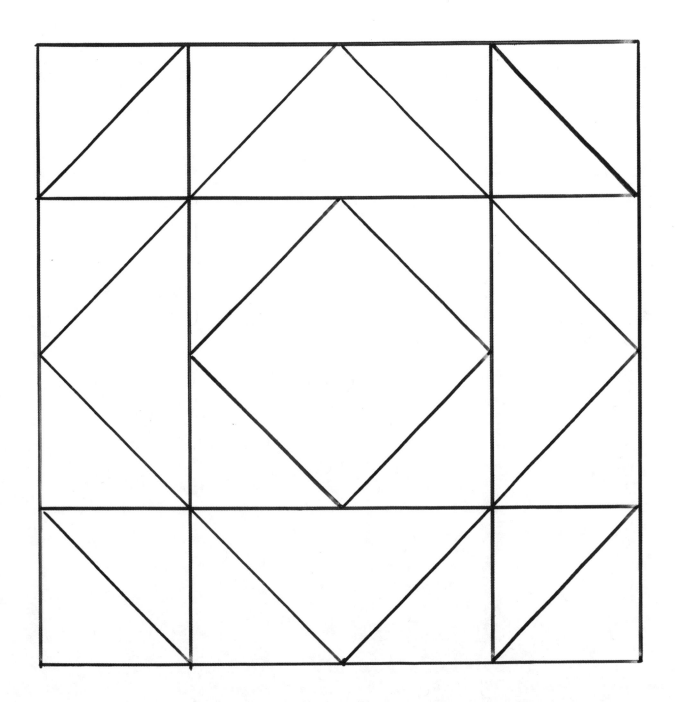

Quilt Template 2

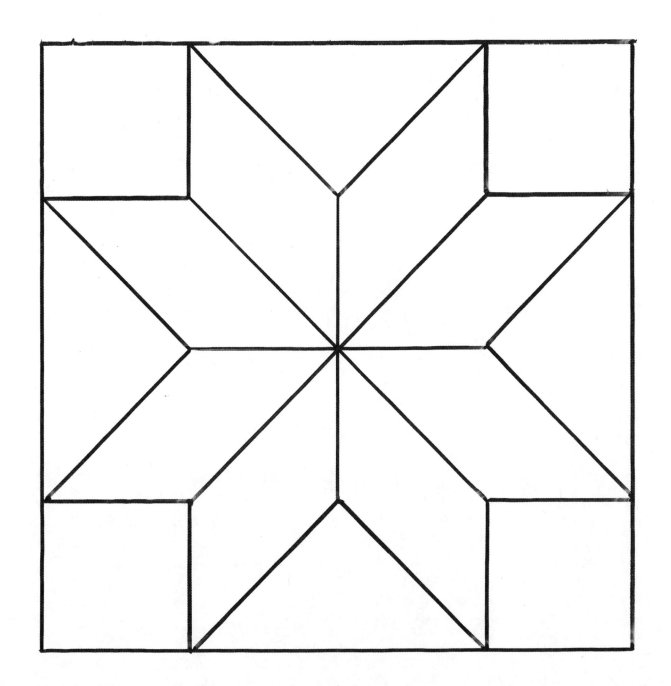

Quilt Template 3

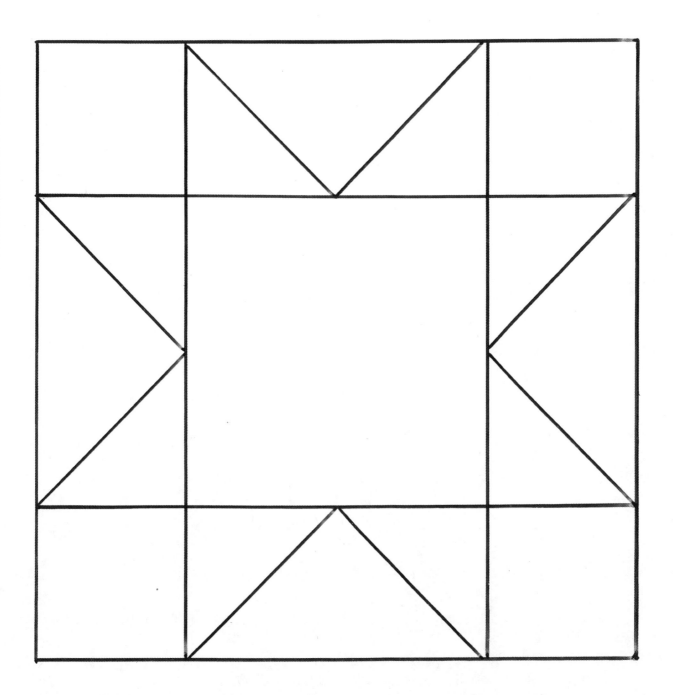

Quilt Template 4

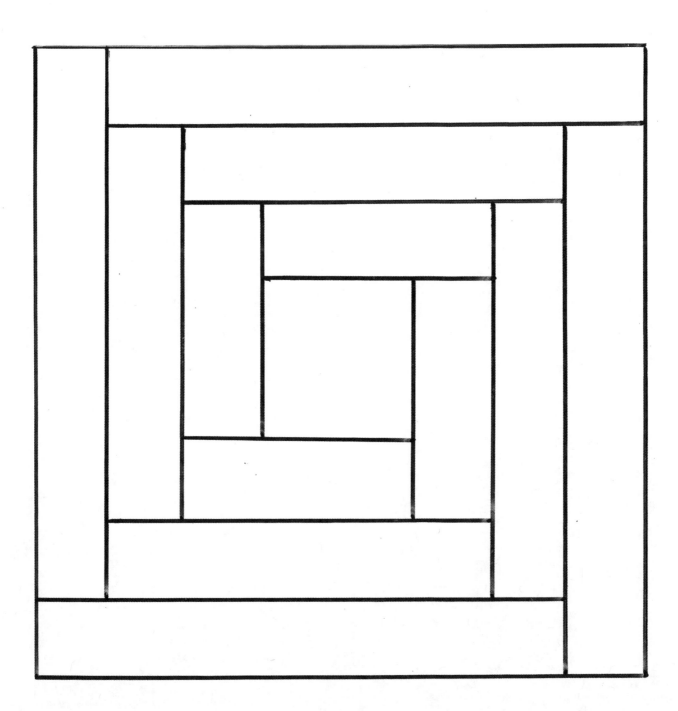

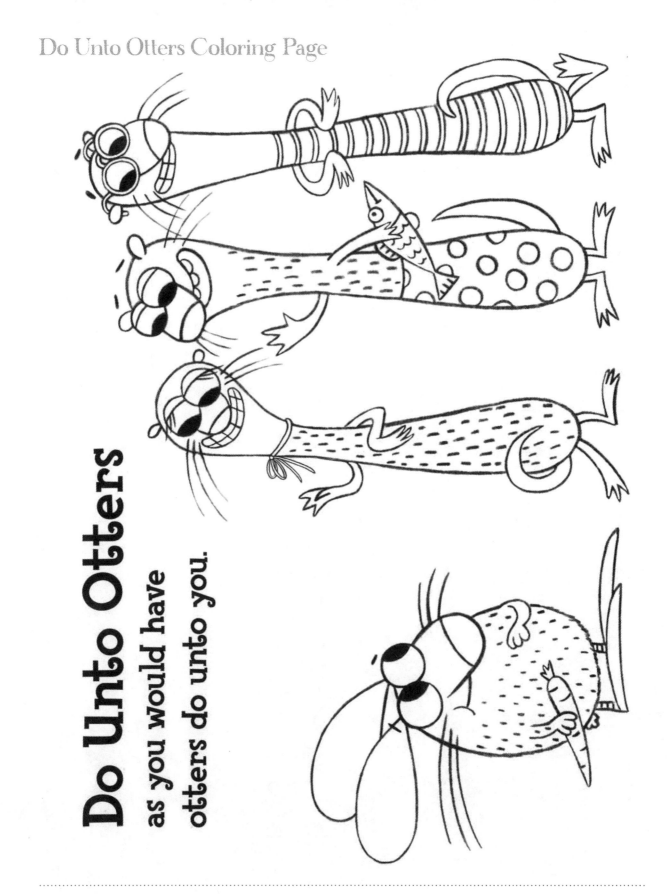

Do Unto Otters

as you would have otters do unto you.

Do Unto Otters Word Search

DOO DEE DOO
MR. RABBIT
MR. OWL
NEIGHBORS
DO UNTO OTTERS
FRIENDLY
NICE SMILE
CHEERFUL HELLO
GOOD EYE CONTACT
POLITE

PLEASE
THANK YOU
EXCUSE ME
NOT LIE
NOT CHEAT
GRACIAS
MERCI
ARIGATO
BITTE
CONSIDERATE

HONEST
KEEP PROMISES
KIND
COOPERATE
PLAY FAIR
SHARE
DON'T TEASE
APOLOGIZE
FORGIVING

```
N O T C H E A T G R A C I A S O
C D Y N V E F O R G I V I N G O
H O K E E P P R O M I S E S O D
E N N I C E S M I L E J M A O E
E T E G N A T I N E O D R R D E
R T X H C D P H C O N I O N E D
F E C B O S T O A E T D W I Y O
U A U O N N I M L N E L L E E O
L S S R S W E E R O K N I Y C D
H E E S I H S S H R G Y K E O A
E T M B D A A A T K A I O L N R
L T E K E R O R N O T B Z U T I
L I W L R Y C M E R C I B E A G
O B P V A P L A Y F A I R I C A
D O U N T O O T T E R S X I T T
C O O P E R A T E P O L I T E O
```

Patience Maze Level 2

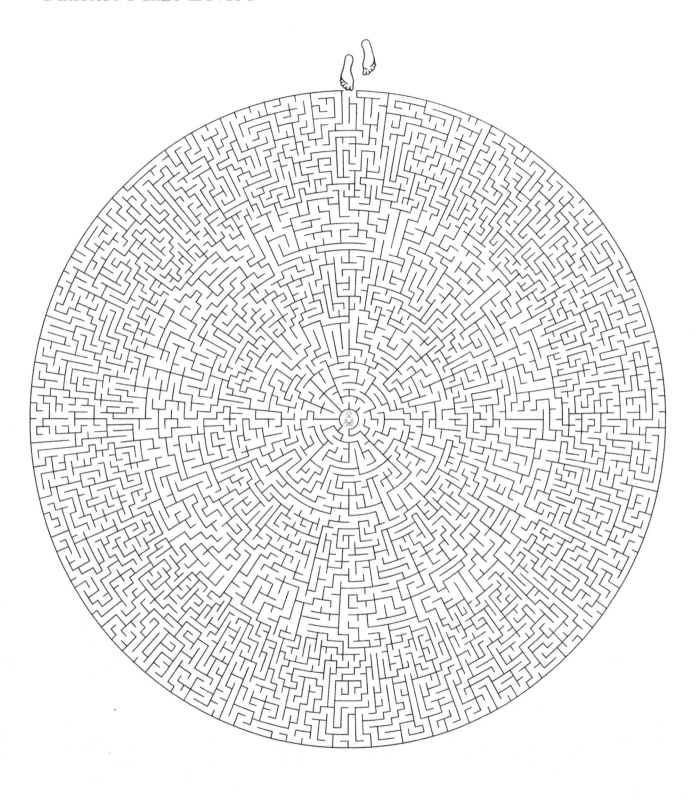

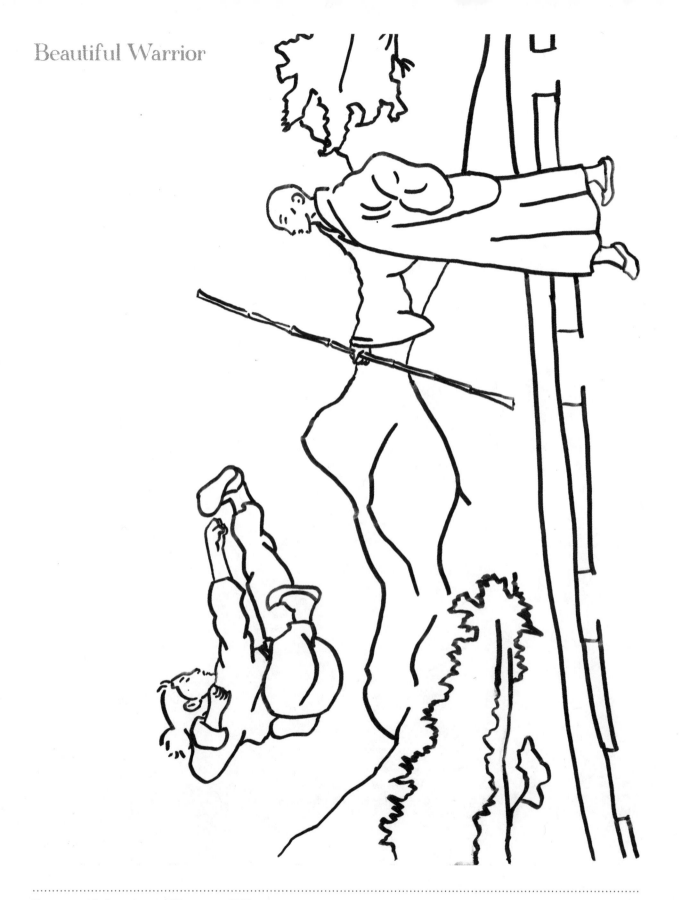

Lotus Craft Template

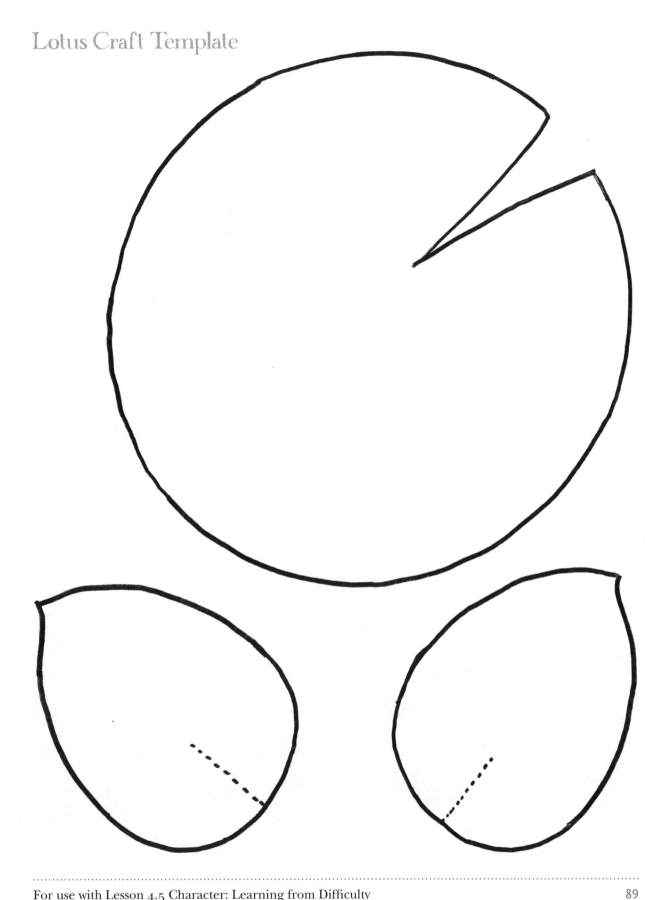

Lotus Pond

Three Wisdom Symbols

Directions: To use this page as an activity, see directions in Lesson 4.6.

Can also be used as a coloring page.

Hand Posture for Meditation

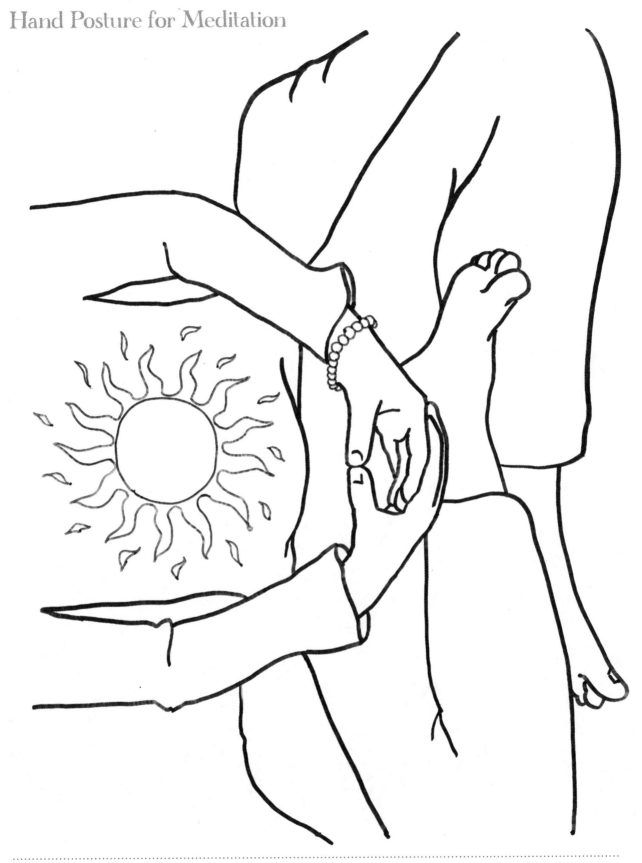

CHARACTER

```
M  W  C  H  A  N  G  E  N  W  K  D
N  E  G  S  U  T  O  L  B  N  N  D
Y  D  D  O  K  Y  I  Z  B  E  R  E
T  T  M  I  L  D  M  M  C  B  Q  Y
R  M  I  L  T  D  Q  N  A  U  G  V
O  O  M  S  J  A  E  X  A  R  D  K
F  D  T  P  O  I  T  N  G  D  A  Y
F  S  V  N  T  R  I  I  R  B  X  P
E  I  Z  A  N  M  E  T  O  U  M  J
Q  W  P  G  I  P  K  N  J  N  L  J
V  B  Y  T  W  Z  P  B  E  L  L  E
Q  R  Y  Q  J  R  T  N  M  G  Y  M
```

GENEROSITY	EQUANIMITY
PATIENCE	LOTUS
MEDITATION	CHANGE
GOLDEN RULE	WISDOM
EFFORT	PARAMITA

The Tree in the Ancient Forest

For use with Lesson 5.1 Nature: Trees & Forests • *Line drawing by the author based on illustration from*
The Tree in the Ancient Forest, *by Carol Reed-Jones and illustrated by Christopher Canyon.*

Trees Crossword

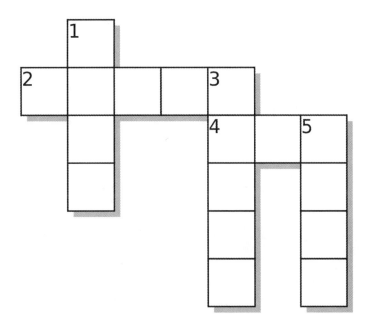

ACROSS

2   Tree product that we write on.

4   Type of bird that lives in trees and eats mice (begins with letter o).

DOWN

1   The "skin" of the tree.

3   Part of tree that's in the ground.

5   Flat, green part of tree that eats sunlight.

Our Favorite Tree

Buddha Connect the Dots

Gardening

Bodhisattva Glasses Template

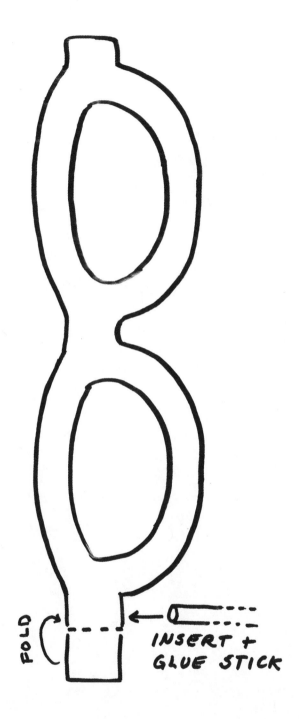

FOLD

INSERT +
GLUE STICK

Trace the Buddha's Face

Peek-a-Buddha

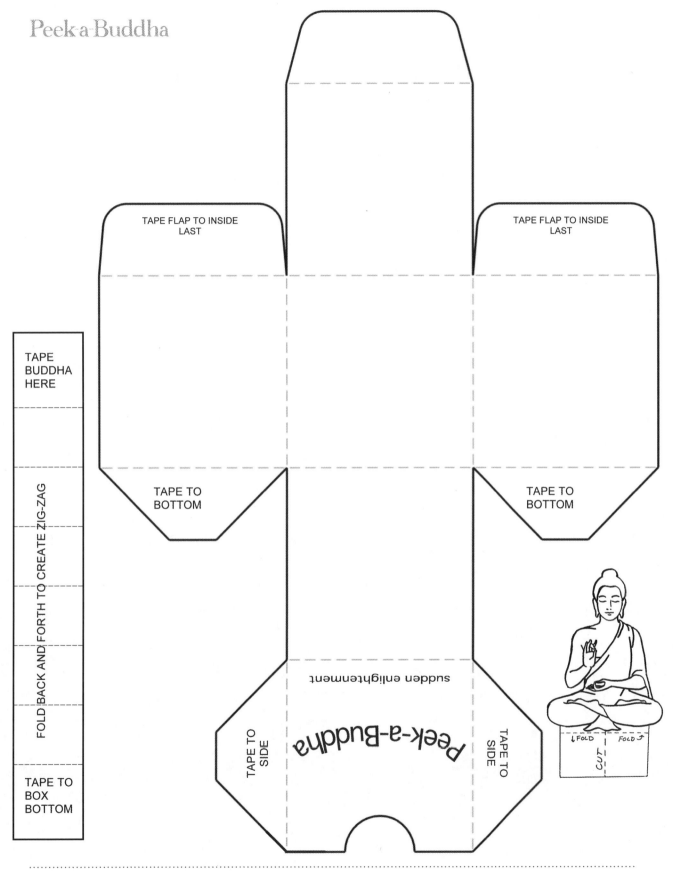

TAPE FLAP TO INSIDE LAST

TAPE FLAP TO INSIDE LAST

TAPE BUDDHA HERE

FOLD BACK AND FORTH TO CREATE ZIG-ZAG

TAPE TO BOX BOTTOM

TAPE TO BOTTOM

TAPE TO BOTTOM

TAPE TO SIDE

TAPE TO SIDE

sudden enlightenment

Peek-a-Buddha

FOLD

FOLD

CUT

Kitten Meditation

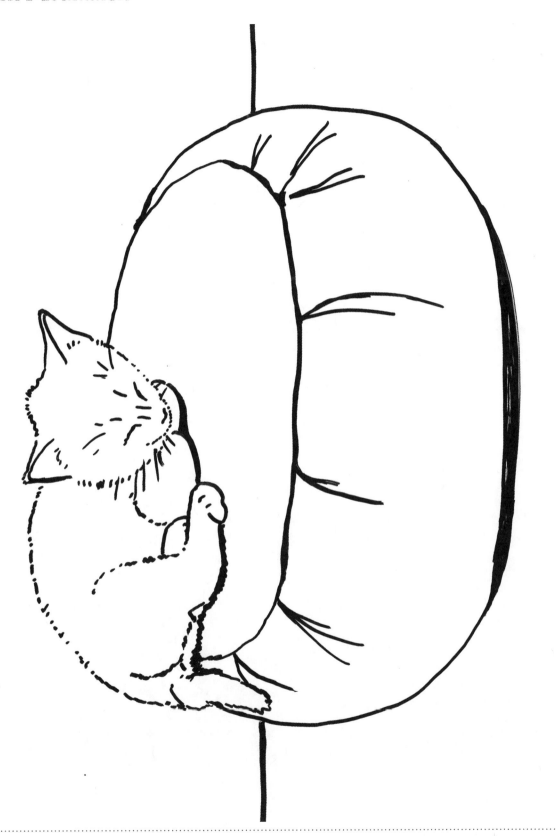

Ethics Worksheet for Adults

To refrain from	Examples of with regards to...	To cultivate	Examples of with regards to...
Killing, harming	Oneself: Relationships: Community:	Compassion, supporting life	Oneself: Relationships: Community:
Stealing, taking what is not given	Oneself: Relationships: Community:	Generosity, sharing, gratitude	Oneself: Relationships: Community:
Sexual misconduct	Oneself: Relationships: Community:	Responsibility with sexual energy, wholesome relationships	Oneself: Relationships: Community:
Speech: lying, divisive speech, harsh speech, gossip	Oneself: Relationships: Community:	Mindful listening and speaking	Oneself: Relationships: Community:
Intoxicants that cloud the mind or impair judgment	Oneself: Relationships: Community:	Consuming healthy foods, ideas, and media	Oneself: Relationships: Community:

5 Guidelines for Speaking

Timely

True

Said Gently

Beneficial

Mind of Goodwill

Directions: Cut out this reminder and post on fridge or wall at home for all to see.

Word Puzzle Answer Keys

ZEN TIES

MOODY COW LEARNS COMPASSION

TREES

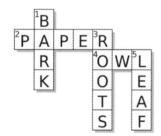

METTA

CHARACTER

MEDITATION WORD SCRAMBLE

HREEATB	BREATHE
AXLRE	RELAX
INMUDLF	MINDFUL
DOYB	BODY
AOTNETITN	ATTENTION
TATIIODMNE	MEDITATION
NAWSERESA	AWARENESS
LAGIKWN	WALKING
BELEPB	PEBBLE
EENPRST	PRESENT
TIEQU	QUIET
ECEULPAF	PEACEFUL

SPEECH WORD SCRAMBLE

TUTHR	TRUTH
LSEI	LIES
SIOGPS	GOSSIP
SPAEEL	PLEASE
OSYENTH	HONESTY
NSEIELC	SILENCE
PNSICSOAOM	COMPASSION
ESIW	WISE
TLOEEENHP	TELEPHONE
SHNGIRA	SHARING

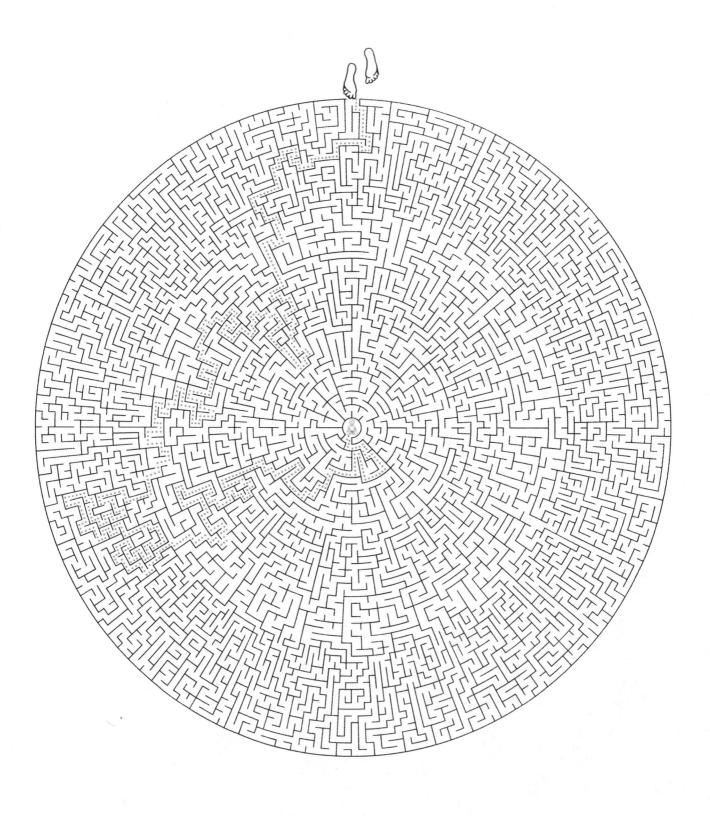

About the Author

PHOTO BY KIM WINTON

SUMI LOUNDON KIM is the founder of and teacher for the Buddhist Families of Durham, and is the Buddhist chaplain at Duke University. Following a master's in Buddhist studies from Harvard Divinity School, she was the associate director for the Barre Center for Buddhist Studies. She has published two books, *Blue Jean Buddha* (2001) and *The Buddha's Apprentices* (2005). Sumi and her husband, a native of South Korea and associate professor at Duke University, live in Durham, North Carolina, with their two children.

For more information, please see wisdompubs.org/sitting-together.

What to Read Next from Wisdom Publications

Sitting Together
A Family-Centered Curriculum on Mindfulness, Meditation & Buddhist Teachings
Adult Study Guide, Children's Lesson Plan
Sumi Loundon Kim

"A wonderful and deeply needed contribution to contemporary life: Sumi Loundon Kim knows her material from the inside out and conveys it in a caring, direct, fun-filled voice. I suspect this work will not only bring well-being to families and communities, it will bring great joy as well."—Sharon Salzberg, author of *Lovingkindness*

Moody Cow Meditates
Kerry Lee MacLean

"Teaching children to meditate might be as easy as herding any other group of frisky critters. *Moody Cow Meditates* fills a distinct void in kid literature."—*Publishers Weekly*

Moody Cow Learns Compassion
Kerry Lee MacLean

One of *Spirituality & Practice*'s Best Spiritual Books of 2012!

Mindful Monkey, Happy Panda
Lauren Alderfer and Kerry Lee MacLean

"This beautiful story shows us all how to dwell peacefully and happily in the present moment."
—Thich Nhat Hanh

No Ordinary Apple
A Story About Eating Mindfully
Sara Marlowe and Philip Pascuzzo

"Deliciously fun to read."—Sharon Salzberg, author of *Lovingkindness*

When the Anger Ogre Visits
Andree Salom and Ivette Salom

"Highly recommended. The content is very practical, and the illustrations (by Ivette Salom) are colorful and entertaining."—*Wildmind Buddhist Meditation*

My New Best Friend
Sara Marlowe and Ivette Salom

"Delightful and charming! This book shows how to be compassionate toward ourselves—encouraging, comforting, forgiving, and supporting ourselves when we need it the most." —Christopher Germer, PhD, author of *The Mindful Path to Self-Compassion*

Zen and Bodhi's Snowy Day
Gina Bates Brown and Sarah Jane Hinder

"Gentle word choice leads young readers from page to page while the cute illustrations evoke peacefulness. Ages three and up."—*ForeWord Reviews*

Prince Siddhartha
The Story of Buddha
Jonathan Landaw and Janet Brooke

"A must-have on the list of any parent interested in exposing a child to the basics of Buddhism."
—*Beliefnet.com*

Prince Siddhartha Coloring Book
Lara Brooke, Janet Brooke, and Jonathan Landaw

A wonderful companion to *Prince Siddhartha*. Includes over 60 illustrations.

Mishan's Garden
James Vollbracht and Janet Brooke

"Quietly compelling storytelling with vivid watercolor portraits of village life."—*Publishers Weekly*

About Wisdom Publications

Wisdom Publications is the leading publisher of classic and contemporary Buddhist books and practical works on mindfulness. To learn more about us or to explore our other books, please visit our website at wisdompubs.org or contact us at the address below.

Wisdom Publications
199 Elm Street
Somerville, MA 02144 USA

We are a 501(c)(3) organization, and donations in support of our mission are tax deductible.

Wisdom Publications is affiliated with the Foundation for the Preservation of the Mahayana Tradition (FPMT).